T.E. LAWRENCE:
HIS ORDERS, DECORATIONS
AND MEDALS

Ronald D. Knight

To my wife Iris, who has faithfully followed me along the T. E. Lawrence trail, with my earnest hope that she has derived some not insignificant enjoyment from our shared experiences.

Also by the Author:

THOMAS HARDY O.M. AND SIR EDMUND GOSSE LITT.D.
(First edition 1968; second revised edition 1978)
HAMBLEDON'S CRICKET GLORY Series: Volumes 2-19 & 26-28
(1974 - 2001 discontinued)
THE KNIGHT FAMILY 'JOURNAL' [Quarterly] (1979-1986 discontinued)
COLONEL T. E. LAWRENCE (Lawrence of Arabia) VISITS MR. & MRS.
THOMAS HARDY (1985)
T. E. LAWRENCE AND THE MAX GATE CIRCLE
(First edition 1988; second revised edition 1995)
T. E. LAWRENCE: HIS ORDERS, DECORATIONS AND MEDALS (1989)
THE HOME FRONT Life in Dorset 1939-1944 (An Evacuee's Experience)
(1999)
T. E. LAWRENCE'S IRISH ANCESTRY AND RELATIONSHIP TO SIR
WALTER RALEIGH (2000)

First Edition 1989
Second (Revised) Edition 2006

© Ronald D. Knight 2006

Published by the author:
Ronald D. Knight
18 Manor Road
Redlands, Weymouth
Dorset DT3 5HR
United Kingdom

ISBN: 0-903769-20-4
978-0-903769-20-4

CONTENTS

PREFACE & ACKNOWLEDGEMENTS TO FIRST EDITION 2
PREFACE & ACKNOWLEDGEMENTS TO SECOND (REVISED) EDITION. 2
THE PUZZLE OF T.E.LAWRENCE:HIS ORDERS, DECORATIONS AND
MEDALS ... 4
CARCHEMISH 6
EARLY WAR SERVICE 8
THE ARAB REVOLT AND DESERT CAMPAIGN 15
AFTER THE DESERT CAMPAIGN 29
POSTSCRIPT 37
BIBLIOGRAPHY 38
THE T.E.LAWRENCE SOCIETY 39

ILLUSTRATIONS:

Front cover: Lawrence's certain awards
Back cover: Lawrence's spurious awards

(between pages 18-19)

Lawrence's certain awards
Lawrence's spurious awards
Citation of Lawrence's 'Légion D'Honneur'
Certificate of a 'Légion D'Honneur'
King George V and Lord Stamfordham
Captain Brodie's 'Order of the Nahda' Citation
Thomas Hardy's 'Order of Merit', etc.
Author wearing Lawrence's certain and spurious awards

PREFACE AND ACKNOWLEDGEMENTS
TO THE FIRST EDITION

This publication originally started off as a talk, which I first gave at Tremadog in North Wales, on the occasion of the T.E.Lawrence Society's gathering there at Easter 1988, to commemorate the centenary of Lawrence's birth. The talk was illustrated by the display of appropriate medals, etc. on a model made up with an R.A.F. uniform tunic to give it some mock authenticity.

The talk has since been repeated, and each time I have been asked for a transcript, which led me to consider publishing it in some permanent form. In addition much further information has since been researched and discovered, and additional appropriate decorations obtained. Hence this eventual illustrated monograph.

My particular study of Lawrence has been his post-war period, especially his friendship with the Dorset novelist and poet - Thomas Hardy, and his wife Florence. This side-tracked interest in Lawrence's decorations came about by chance, as will be explained.

In providing information about, and the obtaining for me of the various items mentioned and illustrated in this publication, I should like to acknowledge assistance received from: Stephen Wheeler of London (dealer in orders, medals and other military items); and similarly Vernon Henstridge of 'Sterling Coins' in Bournemouth, and 'Blade and Bayonet' also of Bournemouth; Iain Duncan (for Hejaz railway photo); Mrs. M. McCann (concerning Captain Brodie); Suleiman Mousa of Jordan; G. W. Nichols; Arthur Russell; the Military Attaché's Office at the Italian Embassy in London; National Museum of the Legion of Honour, Paris; and the Military Secretary, Ministry of Defence, London. I would also thank all those authors and publishers whose books and publications I have quoted from.

Any corrections and further information regarding the subject of this monograph would be greatly appreciated.

Ronald D. Knight   Weymouth
                                                                     Dorset
                                                                 August 1989

PREFACE AND ACKNOWLEDGEMENTS
TO THE SECOND (REVISED) EDITION

The first limited edition of this monograph quickly sold out, but being a somewhat esoteric subject of Lawrence's life, a reprint was not contemplated. However, there have been subsequent enquiries up until the present time as to the possibility of obtaining copies; and it has been seen what prices for a copy can be reached on an internet auction site. Finally, in response to the author's request in the earlier Preface, some helpful additional information and comment was forthcoming. Thus this interest in the subject could now be thought sufficient reason for a reprint.

In the intervening years there has of course been the onset of the world wide web, with its increasing store of information (though to be treated with some caution). One extremely useful instance of this is *The London Gazette*, with editions dating from 1900 now able to be freely accessed, downloaded, and printed-off. Biographies of the whole of Lawrence's life, or specialising in one or more facets, continue to be published, often with fresh insights or information. One or two of these have been helpful in the preparation of this particular publication - see the extended BIBLIOGRAPHY.

There are several reasons to warrant calling it a revised edition: one being that it has been reset, with hopefully greater clarity of illustrations. There has been included the odd factual and spelling correction to the first edition, plus the additional material. There has been particularly included some discussion on the speculation that Lawrence had been awarded the Egyptian 'Order of the Nile', for which the author gratefully thanks Nigel Gage for bringing the appropriate references to his attention. The author again thanks other helpful correspondents, including Ken Divall and George R. Williams; and the various research facilities of The National Archives (previously Public Record Office) at Kew.

Ronald D. Knight   Weymouth
                                                                         Dorset
                                                                      March 2006

THE PUZZLE OF T. E. LAWRENCE'S
ORDERS, DECORATIONS AND MEDALS

Inside both the front and back covers of the author's 1937 copy of *T.E.LAWRENCE BY HIS FRIENDS*, a previous owner had glued in several old newspaper cuttings. An unidentified and undated one read:

TOO MODEST

Sergeant Who Dismissed
Lawrence of Arabia

An amusing story of Aircraftman Shaw
(Col. Lawrence of Arabia) is now
going the rounds of Royal Air Force
messes.
  At a recent full-dress parade Shaw
appeared without wearing medals, and
was reprimaned by a sergeant-major,
who dismissed him from the parade and
ordered him to put on his medals.
  Shaw reappeared with his tunic
almost hidden by medals and Eastern
decorations.
  The remarks of the sergeant-major are
best unrecorded.

If correct, (supposing newspapers in the 1920's and 30's to be as truthful and accurate as they are today!), this incident raises several questions. When and where would this likely to have occurred, and what were all those medals and decorations?

Firstly, to decide the when and where. Lawrence did not adopt the name 'Shaw' until he joined the Tank Corps (at Bovington, in Dorset) in March 1923. Thus the incident referred to seems to have been within his second period of service in the Royal Air Force. This commenced in August 1925, when he transferred from the recently re-named Royal Tank Corps to the R.A.F. College at Cranwell, in Lincolnshire. Whether the said sergeant-major was aware or not of the true identity of 'Shaw', we might assume that it was soon after Lawrence's arrival at the 'spit-and-polish' atmosphere of Cranwell - before he went to India at the end of 1926, and his subsequent enforced return early in 1929 to the more relaxed

R.A.F. Cattewater (later Mount Batten), Plymouth, Devon.

Lawrence recorded something of his early days at Cranwell, in the final chapters of his posthumously published *THE MINT*: but there is no mention of the above episode - for obvious reasons as will be made clear later. However, he did write on page 181 that to his and his fellow aircraftmens' other duties:

'Add, much grudged, an occasional hour wasted over equipment or bayonet for some posh parade: . . .'

R.A.F. tunics at that time were fastened at the neck, and having a belt. However, the peaked caps have remained more or less unchanged, though cap badges have altered as regards the style of crown, which then would have incorporated the contemporary 'Georgian crown'. For photographs of Lawrence in Army and R.A.F. uniform one cannot do better than refer to Tabachnick and Matheson's *IMAGES OF LAWRENCE*.

Having now more or less settled on the possible 'when' and 'where', that is during the Cranwell period, we are left with the 'what' of the various medals and Eastern decorations. This has not been easy to determine. There are apparently no known photographs that show Lawrence with appropriate ribbons on any of his Army and R.A.F. uniforms, let alone any medals and decorations themselves. And Lawrence's close friends at Bovington, Arthur Russell for instance, and Alex Dixon (in his *TINNED SOLDIER* reminscences), have both since confirmed that Lawrence certainly never wore any ribbons or medals whilst stationed there. British Army Records will only give out specific information with the permission of the family. This permission would not be forthcoming in the author's case, who has thus had to rely to a large extent on National Archives primary material, and editions of *The London Gazette* available on the internet, and secondary sources published elsewhere.

CARCHEMISH

For a few years prior to WW1, Lawrence had been engaged at the British Museum's archaeological dig at Carchemish, just inside Turkish Asia Minor: with Leonard Woolley being in charge of operations. On the 20th March 1914, both Lawrence and Woolley were instrumental in saving the lives of German construction engineers in charge of the work on the building of the section of the Berlin-Baghdad railway close to Carchemish, This was on the occasion when the native workmen revolted and were about to mob the engineers.

The incident was mentioned in one of Lawrence's *HOME LETTERS* dated 27th March 1914:

'. . . for the German consul employed us officially to make peace for him on the Company's behalf, between the engineers and the Kurds.'

It was later to be more fully detailed by Woolley in his book *DEAD TOWNS AND LIVING MEN*; and also again by Lawrence in his letter of June 1914 to James Elroy Flecker, published as number 72 in the *LETTERS OF T.E.LAWRENCE* by Garnett.

The local British Vice-Consul subsequently sent a despatch to the Foreign Office, commending the bravery of the two men, saying:

'I propose suggesting to the Vali [a term given for the local Turkish governor] that distinguished Ottoman Decorations conferred upon both Mr Woolley and Mr Lawrence, who saved the situation at Jerablus and who have, besides, rendered such signal services to the Ottoman Museum, would serve to materially demonstrate the well-earned gratitude of the Ottoman Government.' (*BACKING INTO THE LIMELIGHT* by Yardley)

Then in another of his *HOME LETTERS*, dated 1st April 1914, Lawrence just commented:

'We have received the thanks of the Turkish Goverment for settling the Kurd-German dispute of last week.'

Although Woolley also mentioned later that the Turkish Vali just thanked them for what they did, Lawrence later passed on to both his biographers, Robert Graves and Basil Liddell Hart, that he and Woolley were offered Turkish decorations for their share in this episode, but refused. Lawrence again mentioned this offer in *HOME LETTER* dated 8th May 1914, saying;

'*Stupid nonsense: we refused decorations from the Turkish Gov. They are such expensive things!*'

What might then have been offered? In his somewhat unreliable book *WITH LAWRENCE IN ARABIA*, the American journalist Lowell Thomas stated that:

'. . . Lawrence and Woolley arrived on the scene in time to prevent a massacre. As a result of their heroism both archæologists were awarded the Turkish order of the Medjidieh by the Sultan.'

This is a civil and military order of merit, of five classes, founded in 1852 by Sultan Abdul Medjid, which has been widely awarded to British personnel on several occasions.

Suspended from a crimson ribbon having a thin green vertical band close to either edge, is a gold and crimson enamelled star and crescent; from which is further suspended a convex 2-inch wide bronze medal with seven groups of rays, with a star and crescent between each group, superimposed over which is a red enamelled circlet bearing thereon in gold the Turkish for 'zeal, devotion, fidelity', and what would be the equivalent English date of '1852', and in the middle of which is a bronze circle with the Sultan's cypher. On the reverse, in the concavity, is a 'hallmark' or cartouche with an arabic inscription.

It is believed that the illustrated example is of the 5th Class. There is a zig-zag design filed into the back of one of the groups of rays: one theory being that it was to prove that the badge is of silver and not plated.

As Basil Liddell Hart was to write in his '*T.E.LAWRENCE' IN ARABIA AND AFTER*, page 30:

'The Turkish authorities wished to confer decorations . . ., but their offer was declined. In view of the part that T.E. was to play within a few years there would have been a delicious irony in his acceptance.'

G. W. Nichols (see below) obtained confirmation from the Turkish authorities that no record exists of the award of the Order of the Medjidie; but the author's own enquiries seeking details of any supposed offer has never received a reply.

We thus have the first medal that Lawrence did not wear on that unknown newspaper's reported parade.

EARLY WAR SERVICE

There would have followed in due course his later WW1 general service and campaign medals, awards for gallantry, and decorations for meritorious service.

To determine the first group it was necessary to know the dates and locations of his army service. Thankfully, much of this had already been basically researched and covered by G. W. Nichols in his article 'SOME NOTES ON THE MILITARY CAREER OF T.E.LAWRENCE' in the *T.E.Lawrence Studies NEWSLETTER*, Vol. 1, No. 2, 1981-2.

War was declared against Germany by Britain on 4th August 1914. Apparently Lawrence was later initially to work for a few days as a civilian at the War Office in London. Then in the *Third Supplement to The London Gazette*, number 28964, of 5th November 1914, page 9004, there was announced:

'The undermentioned to be temporary Lieutenants:-
T. G. Lawrence, to be temporary Second Lieutenant. Dated 23rd October, 1914'

Subsequently in *The London Gazette*, number 28977, of 17th November 1914, page 9409, there was a correction:

'The name of Temporary Second Lieutenant T. E. Lawrence is as now described, and not as stated in the Gazette of 5th November, 1914.'

The *Army List* for December 1914 confirmed this appointment as:

'23-10-1914 2nd Lt. Interpreter. War Office.'

He would have previously obtained his appropriate qualifying certificates whilst in the Oxford University Officers Training Corps. He continued to be employed in the Geographical Section at the War Office, until his departure for Egypt on 9th December. He would thus not have qualified for the '1914 Star', awarded for early service with the British Expeditionary Force in France and Belgium.

On arrival in Egypt he joined the new Military Intelligence Department in Cairo, gathering and disseminating intelligence about the Turks who had entered the war on 29th October, on the side of Germany. He was to be employed making appropriate reports and maps, and questioning Turkish prisoners.

The *London Gazette*, number 29063, dated 9th February 1915, page 1324, contained the following entry amongst the appointments:

'Commands And Staff
Staff Captains-
Temporary Second Lieutenant T. E. Lawrence. Dated 15th December, 1914.'

This latter date was the day following his arrival in Cairo. To go fully into details of Lawrence's uniforms, badges, etc. is too big a subject to include in this particular study, (and has already warranted some separate research by the author, the results of which he has also presented in draft manuscript form to the Library of the T.E.Lawrence Society).

Lawrence transferred to the high-powered Arab Bureau when it was formed on 1st January 1916. According to *THE SECRET LIVES OF LAWRENCE OF ARABIA* by Knightley and Simpson, page 48, it was to be impressed upon the armed forces that:

'temporary naval or military rank held by officials of the Bureau is in no way indicative of their political status or duties.'

Lawrence's future roles were to bear out this injunction.
On 18th March 1916 he had been cited by:

'Le President de la Republique Française,
Sur la propositiondu President du Conseil,
Ministre des Affaires Etrangéres,
Décrète:
Art. 1er-Sont nommés dans l'Ordre National de la Legion d'Honneur les Officiers de l'armée Britannique ci aprés désignés:
. . . .
2^0-au grade de Chevalier.
. . . .
17463 M.le Lieutenant T. E. Lawrence, du Service des Renseignement au Caire.
[i.e. for Intelligence Service in Cairo]

Art. II - Le President du Conseil, Ministre des Affaires Etrangéres, et le Grand Chancelier de l'Ordre sont chargés, chacun en ce qui le concerne, de l'exécution du présent décret.

Fait à *Paris*, le *18 Mars* 1916
Signé: *R. Poincaré*
Contresigné: *A. Briand*'

A 'Chevalier' is the 5th and lowest rank of the Order. According to a letter of reply to the author, dated 28th December 1987, from the Musée National de la Légion d'Honneur, at 2 Rue de Bellechasse, Paris VIIe, the medal is a:

'Ten pointed, gold rimmed, white enamel star with a gold ballon the tip of each point. The rays of the star are united by wreaths of oak and laurel leaves. The center medallion is gold and portrays profile of laurel crowned female, symbolizing the French Republic, surrounded by a gold rimmed blue band inscribed in gold lettering REPUBLIQUE FRANCAISE 1870. On the reverse are crossed French flags in natural colors on a gold background [surrounded] by a gold edged blue band with the inscription HONNEUR ET PATRIE. The badge is suspended from an oval green and gold enamel laurel and oak wreath.
The Legion of Honor was established by Napoleon Bonaparte on May 19, 1802 as an award to French citizens and Foreigners, male or female for outstanding services, civil or military, on behalf of France.'

The whole of the medal is hung from a scarlet ribbon. The badge is not marked with the name of the recipient. Unfortunately enamel is liable to chipping, as the illustrated example of the award shows.
Also on the above Citation is the notation:

'*transmit* 17 MAI 1916'

which might mean the date when sending off of the respective decoration and/or Citation. But in the National Archives, under reference numbers FO 372/835 & 836, there is a letter dated 30th April 1916 from the French Ambassador to the British Foreign Office, expressing the President of the Republic of France's decision to confer the Legion of Honour upon several British personnel, including Lawrence. There is also a copy of the Ambassador's covering letter to the Foreign Office, dated 20th June 1916, which accompanied the several Certificates which were to be sent to the respective recipients. One wonders what eventually happened to Lawrence's Certificate, but illustrated is part of one issued to another recipient in 1920.
A recipient of this award can wear a small narrow red clip in the left lapel button-hole. That it is still a current practice is borne out with the instance of a 101-year old ex-Royal Flying Corps veteran who was a member of the Weymouth Branch of The Royal British Legion. He qualified for the French general distribution (around the year 2000) of the Legion of Honour to living British WW1 survivors. The author advised him about the additional lapel insignia, which he was able to obtain apparently without difficulty, and

subsequently wore it with pride.

An announcement of this '*Croix de Chevalier*' being conferred upon:

'Temp. 2nd Lt. Thomas Edward Lawrence, Spec. List.'

was published in the Second Supplement to *The London Gazette* number 29584, dated 16th May 1916, page 4936.

The 'Special List' was a convenient category to cover officers with no regimental attachment.

The Sovereign's subjects are not permitted to accept and wear the insignia of an Order or Decoration of a foreign country or of a Commonwealth country of which the Sovereign is not the Head of State, unless permission has been granted by the Sovereign. This permission is granted on application to the Secretary of State for Foreign and Commonwealth Affairs with whom the proposal will normally have been cleared in advance, through the diplomatic channels of the government making the award. Permission is granted in one of two ways, namely restricted or unrestricted.

Restricted Permission In this intance, the recipient receives instructions from the Sovereign's Private Secretary regarding the occasions when the insignia may be worn.

Unrestricted Permission This enables Foreign insignia to be worn on all occasions when any British insignia is worn so that decorations and medals which are usually worn from a medal brooch may be mounted permanently after any British Orders, Decorations and Medals. Their order should be based on that listed in the Order of Precedence, i.e. Orders, then Decorations, then Medals in order of date award.

It is generally accepted that if any members of the armed forces who are serving for an extended period of time in an overseas force and receive Orders, Decorations and Medals from that particular country where they are serving, then those items should take precedence over any British Orders, Decorations and Medals while serving in that country or subsequently, on any occasion connected with that country.

Thus in *The London Gazette*, number 29600, dated 30th May 1916, page 5321, appeared the following notice:

'The KING has been pleased to give and grant unto the undermentioned Officers His Majesty's Royal licence and authority to wear Decorations (as stated against their respective names) which have been conferred upon them by the President of the French Republic in recognition of valuable services rendered by them:-

Chevalier of the Legion of Honour
Temporary Captain Thomas Edward Lawrence, Special List.'

The *Army List Supplement* for July 1916 named him as an officer authorised to wear foreign decorations on all occasions. So far the author has not come across any direct reference to any actual presentation to, or receipt by Lawrence of the award.

It was ironic that he should be awarded this decoration, in view of his apparent antagonism to French colonial aspirations in the Middle East. On the other hand, following Lawrence's future war record, it might be considered that he ought to have later been awarded at least the next higher class of this award - that of 'Officer'! This award was also ironic in view of the 'dishonourable' mission he was being sent on later in the March.

In the *Third Supplement to The London Gazette* number 29632, of 21st June 1916, page 6185, was published a Despatch dated 16th March 1916 from General Sir John Maxwell, the Commander of the Force in Egypt. Amongst those whom he wished to bring to the notice of the War Office 'in connection with Administration in Egypt' was:

'GENERAL LIST
Temp. 2nd Lt. T. E. Lawrence, Intell.'

A medal card for Lawrence (later passed to the National Archives) was accordingly made out:

'Lawrence, T.E. 2nd Lieut Intelligence General List M.I.D. L.G. 21.6.16. Page 6185'

The National Archives reference no. FO 372/832 had actually listed

'for services in connection with military operations in Egypt. . . .
Second Lieutenant T. E. Lawrence, Intelligence Department: another Archaeologist [with Second Lieutenant Wooley (sic)] with intimate knowledge of Asia Minor and Syria was of the greatest possible use in the Map Section and in interviewing all refugees or prisoners from Arabia or Asia Minor.'

In *The London Gazette*, number 29552, of 18th April 1916, page 4026, was the announcement:

'Memoranda.
Temp. 2nd Lt. T. E. Lawrence to be temp. Capt. whilst specially employed. 20th
Mar. 1916.'

This promotion to Captain (as distinct presumably from any Staff Captaincy) is
thought to have been to allow him more authority to assist as part of a delegation
in negotiating (with the aid of bribes) with the Turkish commander who had a
large British force under seige at Kut-el-Amara in Mesopotamia. This surmise
was borne out by Lawrence's own reply to a question later asked by his
biographer Liddell Hart:

'I was Staff Captain. I lost it on going to Mespot, so Hedley arranged a local
captaincy.'

- see *T. E. LAWRENCE TO HIS BIOGRAPHER: LIDDELL HART*, page 62;
and GRO List 97 which showed him as

'Temporary Captain on Special Duties'.

These negotiations, which were to prove more or less unsuccessful, and other
matters, took Lawrence away from Cairo for some three months.
    He later relinquished the rank of Captain with cessation of employment as a
Staff Captain on reorganisation in Cairo (List 226 of 19th November 1916). He
thus seemingly reverted back to being a Lieutenant, for he was to be addressed as
such in an official note concerning his report of his meeting with Arab leaders in
late 1916, a few months after the start of the Arab Revolt.
    In June 1990, as a result of reading the earlier edition of this monograph,
T.E.Lawrence Society member Nigel Gage kindly brought to the attention of the
author a passage in *THE DIARIES OF PARKER PASHA*, edited by
H.V.Winstone. On page 158 was the following comment by Parker:

'Master Wingate [General Wingate] was now in absolute charge and his own
favourite sons were taking over. He had little time for Parker and much for
Lawrence, for whom he had engineered the *Order of the Nile* (for map work) in
September [1916]. FO 372/832'

    Subsequent investigation by the author determined that Winstone (or his
researcher) had apparently misinterpreted official documents in the then Public
Record Office (now National Archives). It would seem that Wingate only
"enquired" about a possible award to Lawrence. His name was not to be found

amongst the few British servicemen considered and agreed to receive this Order in FO372/832, which relates to General Correspondence - Treaty, Egypt 1916 Files 117896-263298. Nor was his name able to be found in *The London Gazette* amongst the names of those British personnel eventually awarded the Order of the Nile. (Fuller details of this investigation may be found in a separate manuscript by the author donated to the T.E.Lawrence Society's Library.) Two enquiries to the Embassy of the Arab Republic of Egypt in London failed to receive any replies.

This Order of the Nile was instituted in 1915 by the Sultan of Egypt for rewarding persons who had rendered useful service to that country, including many British Officer serving in Egypt. There were five classes, with the lowest being the 'Chevalier'. The badge was formed of ten points or rays, having in its centre a five-pointed star of white enamel. In the centre of this, on azure enamel, was an Egyptian inscription which translated said "What benefits Egypt owes to the Nile, her source of prosperity and happiness!" It was worn on the left breast, being hung from its ribbon by a crown. The ribbon was of sky-blue, with a narrow yellow band near each edge.

On the 19th October 1916, Colonel Parker was to make reference in his *Diary* to:

'Captain Lawrence.'

THE ARAB REVOLT AND DESERT CAMPAIGN

The Arab Revolt against the Turks had been started by Grand Sherif Hussein of Mecca in June 1916. Lawrence first went to Arabia in the October to begin his liaison with Emir Feisal and the Arab forces, in what was to be known as the Desert Campaign, so brilliantly chronicled in the *Seven Pillars of Wisdom*. This Campaign was to finally end in October 1918 with the capture of Damascus.
In the *Arab Bulletin* No. 37, of 4th January 1917, Lawrence is referred to as:

'Captain Lawrence.'

Also, in one of his *HOME LETTERS* from Cairo, that dated 25th February 1917, he wrote:

'I have now been made a Captain and Staff Captain again, which is amusing. It doesn't make any difference of course really, as I am never in uniform in Arabia, and nobody cares a straw what rank I hold, except that I am of Sherif Feisul's household.'

The *Second Supplement to The London Gazette*, number 30218, of 4th August 1917, page 8001, then announced:

'Memoranda.
Temp. Capt. T. E. Lawrence to be temp. Maj. 5th Aug. 1917.'

Later in *HOME LETTER* dated 27th August 1917 he was to point out that he had now returned to the Egyptian Expeditionary Force, and was no longer with the Arab Bureau.
The *Third Supplement to The London Gazette*, number 30222, 7th August 1917, page 8103, stated:

'The KING has been graciously pleased to give orders for the following appointments to the Most Honourable Order of the Bath, for valuable services rendered in connection with Military Operations in the Field, to be dated 4th June 1917:-
To be Additional Members of the Military Division of the Third Class, or Companions, of the said most Honourable Order:-
Temp. Maj. Thomas Edward Lawrence, Gen. List.'

This appointment as a Companion of the Bath - Military Division, was awarded for the capture of the port of Akaba on 6th July 1917. For this feat he was initially recommended for the Victoria Cross by General Wingate, according to Lawrence (see *T.E.LAWRENCE TO HIS BIOGRAPHERS:GRAVES*). But partly for the reason there was no more senior officer present it could not be awarded. He had also been suggested for the lower Distinguished Service Order. According to Tunbridge in *WITH LAWRENCE IN THE R.A.F.*, on the Ministry of Defence copy of this *Gazette* it is annotated that the D.S.O. award was declined, making reference to file 0127 in 2694: but which file was said not to have survived.

'Companion' is the third and lowest grade of the Order. Recipients wear a smaller-sized Badge than do those of the higher ranks of the Order. This is composed of a rose, thistle and shamrock issuing from a sceptre between three imperial crowns, surrounded by the motto **TRIA JUNCTA IN UNO** ('Three Joined in One'). This, in turn, is surrounded by a laurel wreath on a green circlet, with below a dark blue enamel scroll bearing the words **ICH DIEN** ('I Serve') in gold letters. The Badge is suspended from a crimson ribbon worn round the neck. (The form of ring suspension on the illustrated example indicates that it would have been invested from June 1917 onwards.) The Badge would not be marked with the name of the recipient; and on death of the recipient is not returnable to the Secretary of The Central Chancery of the Orders of Knighthood at St. James's Palace. Its position in the 'Order of Precedence of Orders' is fairly lowly, being about two-thirds of the way down the list.

Even so, one can now begin to see the incongruity of the situation, of a mere aircraftman wearing such honour decorations: something out of all proportion to his now lowly rank, on one of his 'posh' parades, wearing best uniform, puttees and boots.

Lawrence's promotion to Temporary Major is thought to have been as much to fulfill the conditions for the award of the Companion of the Bath, which could only be conferred upon officers the rank of major and above in the army (or commander in the navy) who had been mentioned in despatches for services in war, and that they might subsequently be advanced to the higher grades of the Order (see October/November 1918). A 'Temporary' rank is exactly what it says, with no degree of permanancy but liability to reversion to a lower rank on change of circumstances.

In another of his *HOME LETTERS*, dated 5th September 1917, from Akaba, Lawrence wrote in confirmation:

'Tell mother they asked for that twopenny thing she likes, but fortunately didn't get it. [Victoria Cross] All these letters & things are so many nuisances afterwards, & I'll never wear or use any of them. Please don't, either. My address is simply T.E.L., no titles please.'

And in another from Akaba, on the 24th September 1917, he wrote:

'. . . and for my present don't put either Major or C.B. or any other letters (past present or future) after my name when writing to me . . . I'm sending back all private letters so addressed.'

Then in the *Second Supplement to The London Gazette*, number 30263, dated 31st August 1917, pages 9102/9103, was:

'War Office, *31st August, 1917.*
The following is among the Decorations and Medals awarded by the Allied Powers at various dates to the British Forces for distinguished services rendered during the course of the campaign:-
His Majesty has given unrestricted permission in all cases to wear the Decorations and Medals in question.
Decorations and Medals conferred by
HIS MAJESTY THE KING OF ITALY
Silver Medal for Military Valour
Temporary 2nd Lieutenant Thomas Edward Lawrence, Special List.'

(Note the still lowly substantive rank!)
This award was instituted in 1833, in the three classes of gold, silver and bronze, for gallantry in action. All three are of the same design, the obverse having the Arms of Savoy and two sprays of foliage, surmounted by the crown, and surrounded by the words **AL VALORE MILITAIRE** ('For Military Valour'). The reverse has two circular sprays of laurel, with room for the recipient to insert his name, etc. in the centre (which was a common practice). The ribbon is bright blue, moiré (which means having a watery-looking surface); and when the riband alone is worn, it would for example in Lawrence's case have a silver five-pointed star on it.
As the gold award was considered equivalent to the Victoria Cross, and therefore rarely awarded, the silver could perhaps be equated with the Distinguished Service Order. However, the silver and bronze could be won more than once by any one person; and one reference book even goes so far as to comment that they were given out almost as much as campaign medals. But in *The London Gazette* listings, the Silver is restricted to Officers, whilst the Bronze was awarded to a much longer list of 'other ranks' only (including the author's distant uncle who

had served during the Desert Campaign in the Imperial Camel Corps .
It will be noted that Italy was on the side of the Allies during WW1. It could be assumed that the award had been for Lawrence's part in the capture of Aqaba in the mid-July. Enquiries by the author to the Italian authorities for further informtion brought the following reply in April 1989, from the Military Attaché's Office at the Italian Embassy in London.

'Following further enquiries and research through appropriate Authorities, it emerged that there is no evidence in the Italian records of any decoration being awarded to T.E.Lawrence.

The case was also raised back in 1975 when Lt. Paul Tumbridge, RAF, asked to enquire on the issue and gave as evidence a copy of the Supplement to the London Gazette, 31 August 1917, 9103. Research carried out at the time also produced no results. Perhaps it would be useful for you to find out which documentation supported the announcement in the London Gazette.'

The Ministry of Defence in London was unable to assist further. No efforts were made at the time by the author to search through the National Archives, or to trace Lt. Paul Tumbridge for further information, who has now produced his own relevant publication (see the BIBLIOGRAPHY).

Lawrnce's promotion was further confirmed in a letter which David Hogarth, who was Lawrence's friend, mentor and (as Head of the Arab Bureau in Cairo) also sometime his chief, had written to his (Hogarth's) sister in October 1917, and quoted in *A TOUCH OF GENIUS* by Brown and Cave, page xv.):

'[Lawrence] *is going out again for a spell and [his family]* must not expect letters from him; but whenever I have news of him I'll let them know the facts whether through you or direct. But the intervals will be long. Tell his mother he has now five decorations including the C.B. (to qualify for which he had to be promoted to major) and despises and ignores the lot . . . [H]is reputation has become overpowering.'

So what were these five decorations that Lawrence was said to have by this date? Mention has been only made so far of the gazetted awards of the Legion of Honour, the Companionship of the Bath, and the Silver Medal for Valour.

In the *Seventh Supplement to The London Gazette*, number 30289, of 14th September 1917, page 9645, Lawrence's name appears as:

'*Staff.*
Lawrence, Temp. Capt. T. E., Spec. List.'

Lawrence's certain awards:
Companionship of the Bath (military)
Distinguished Service Order
1914-1915 Star
British War Medal
Victory Medal 1918 with oak leaf
Legion of Honour (Chevalier)
Croix de Guerre with palm
Italian Silver Medal for Military Valour

Lawrence's spurious awards:
Order of Merit (reverse of civil version), Hejaz Order of al Nahda.
Turkish Order of the Medjidie, Iraqi Order of the Two Rivers
(military version)

Le Président de la République Française,

Sur la proposition du Président du Conseil,
Ministre des Affaires Étrangères,

Décrète :

Art. 1er — Sont nommés dans l'Ordre National de la Légion d'Honneur les Officiers de l'armée Britannique ci-après désignés :

1°: — au grade d'Officier

17460 + M. le Lieutenant-Colonel G.F. Clayton, Directeur du Service des Renseignements au Caire ;

2°: — au grade de Chevalier

17461 + M. le Major Stewart F. Newcombe, Commandant le Génie de la 2e Division australienne.

17462 + M. le Capitaine W. Walford, aide de camp du Général Commandant en Chef des Troupes Britanniques d'occupation en Égypte.

17463 + M. le Lieutenant C.E. Lawrence, du Service des Renseignements au Caire.

Art. II _____ Le Président du Conseil, Ministre des Affaires Étrangères, et le Grand Chancelier de l'Ordre sont chargés, chacun en ce qui le concerne, de l'exécution du présent décret.

Fait à Paris, le 18 Mars 1916

Signé : R. Poincaré
Contresigné : A. Briand

Pour ampliation :
Le Ministre Plénipotentiaire, Chef du Service du Protocole,

William ....

Citation of Lawrence's 'Légion D'Honneur'

ORDRE NATIONAL DE LA LÉGION D'HONNEUR.

HONNEUR. PATRIE.

Le Grand Chancelier de l'Ordre National de la Légion d'Honneur

certifie que, par Décret du _____ deux _____ Avril _____ mil neuf cent=vingt

Le Président de la République Française

a conféré au _____ Major Walter Rothney Battye, de l'Armée Britannique ;

D.A.O., M.B., F.R.C.S., Indian Medical Service,

la Décoration de _____ Chevalier _____ de l'Ordre National de la Légion d'honneur :

Fait à Paris, le 12 Avril 1920

Vu, mis à emploi, N° 24.407

Le Chef de 1.er Bureau

King George V and his private secretary Lord Stamfordham

Captain S.H. Brodie's Citation for his Order of al Nahda,
with translation.

Copy

The Hashemite Bureau

The Slave of God
Al-Hussein Ibn Ali.

The truthfulness and sincerity of
Lieut S. H. Brodie, M.C. to our Hashemite
Throne and his valuable services and
righteous endeavours in the Great War
having been proved, we have issued our
Royal decree to confer upon him the
High Order of the "Nahda" as a reward
for his deeds and an appreciation of
his sincerity.

May God grant a good reward to Benefactors!
Issued this 9th day of Moharram, 1338

Thomas Hardy's Order of Merit, Watch and Prize Medallion

Author wearing Lawrence's certain and spurious awards

amongst those

'brought to the notice of the Secretary of State for War for valuable services rendered in connection with Military Operations in the Field.'

This was presumably a 'Mention in Despatches', and emanated possibly from a Despatch dated 25th June 1917 to the War Office from General Wingate, General Officer Commanding, Hedjaz - which was subsequently published in the *Fifth Supplement to The London Gazette*, number 31690, 12th December 1919, pages 15605/15607. On page 15606 may be read:

'*10. The raiding operations which have been instituted against the enemy's lines of communication have attained a considerable measure of success. . . , and a considerable number of Arabs were trained in demolition work and are now operating under the personal direction of Lieut.-Colonel S. F. Newcombe, D.S.O., R.E., Captain T. E. Lawrence and Lieut. H. Garland.*'

Lawrence's chief, Hogarth, may have had advance notice that on the 23rd November 1917 Lawrence was being further cited for an award by France. This time it was to be with the *Croix de Guerre avec palme*, supposedly for the capture of Aqaba early in the July. National Archives reference no. FO 372/1121 records:

'*Received Jan 15 1918*
Citation accorded Major T. E. Lawrence:
Trs. copy for transmission to recipient. "Croix de Guerre" is being bestowed by Col. Brémond.
Copy to War Office, with orig. encls.'

'*Ambassade De France À Londres.*
    Le Gouvernement Français, désireux de reconnaitre officiellement la brillante conduite du Major Thomas Edward Lawrence de l'Etat-Major du Haut Commissaire du Gouvernement Britannique en Egypte, lui a accordé une citation à l'ordre de l'armée, comportant attribution de la Croix de Guerre avec palme.-Le Colonel Brémond, Chef de la Mission Militaire Française en Egypte, a été désigné pour notifier cette décision au Major Lawrence et lui remettre la Croix de Guerre.-
    L'Ambassadeur de France a l'honneur de transmettre, ci-joint, à M'Balfour copie de la citation dont il s'agit en le priant de bien vouloir la faire parvenir à l'intéressé.

M.Paul Cambon saisit cette occasion pour renouveler au Principal Secrétaire d'Etat pour les Affaires Etrangères les assurances de sa haute considération.

Albert Gate House,
14 Janvier 1918.'

('The French Government, desirous of officially recognising the brilliant conduct of Major Thomas Edward Lawrence . . .,'

and it goes on to say that the decoration was apparently to be bestowed by Colonel Brémond.)

This award was not to be publicly announced until the *Fifth Supplement to The London Gazette*, number 30638, of 18th April 1918, page 4716, when he was listed:

'*Croix de Guerre*

Temporary Major Thomas Edward Lawrence, C.B., Special List.'

Apparently (according to Tunbridge) a French Minister of War telegram, dated 23rd November 1917, had read:

'This senior officer of outstanding merit, has by his personal influence, brought together Arab contingents which have assisted, with him at the head, often without food and water, in carrying out operations of the most daring kind with complete success. Has made many raids on the railway about Maan and captured Akaba.'

Colonel Brémond, who for a time was Head of the French Military Mission in the Hejaz, and with whom Lawrence had continual opposition and struggles during the war, had to draw up the citation, which (according to Yardley's *BACKING INTO THE LIMELIGHT*, page 114) read:

'Le Président du Conseil, Ministre de la Guerre, cite à l'ordre de l'Armée:

LAWRENCE, Thomas Edouard, Major à l'Etat-Major du Haute-Commissaire du Gouvernement Brittanique en Egypte pour le motif suivant:

Officier supérieur de la plus haute valeur. Par son action personelle a su grouper autour de lui contingents bédouins à la tête desquels il a accompli ses opérations de la plus grande audace, avec le succès le plus complet, sans eau et sans ravitaillement, compromettant les communications des troupes turques du Hedjaz.

Paris, le 23 Novembre 1917
Signé: L. Mordacq.'

It will be noticed that for political or other reasons Brémond's citation deliberately omits any direct mention of Aqaba. It was quite probably chagrin, for he had wanted it captured with an Anglo-French force from the sea - q.v. *SEVEN PILLARS OF WISDOM*, chapter XXVIII, 3rd February 1917.

According to Knightley and Simpson's *THE SECRET LIVES OF LAWRENCE OF ARABIA*, page 82, Brémond had also presented the medal - but according to Tunbridge the medal was finally able to be presented to Lawrence by Captain Pisani in early 1918. But Lawrence was to post it back to Brémond just after the Armistice. See below for Lawrence's comments in one of his *HOME LETTERS*, dated 14th December 1917.

This French decoration was instituted in April 1915. The ribbon is dark green with seven thin vertical red stripes; having suspended from it a bronze quartered-cross and two crossed swords. with at the centre a small circle inscribed obversely **REPUBLIQUE FRANCAISE**, and enclosing a female head; and reversely a plain circle enclosing two dates which ranged from **1914 1915** to **1914 1918**. Lawrence's would therefore have been dated either **1914 1917** or **1914 1918** depending to some extent on the date of presentation. The one illustrated is dated **1914 1918**.

The medal is worn with a wide variety of different emblems on the ribbon, depending on the form of mention. It can be worn with a choice of three stars - bronze for a brigade, regimental or unit citation; silver for a divisional citation; and vermilion for an army corps citation. 'With palm' represents an army citational order, and is thus the highest grade of award. The medal is not marked with the recipient's name.

D.G.Hogarth wrote at the time that this was the French equivalent of the Victoria Cross; though the French writer Maurice Larès stated in his article 'T.E.Lawrence and France: Friends or Foes?' in Tabachnick's *THE T.E.LAWRENCE PUZZLE*, page 226, that this award as being for 'a mention in dispatches', as similarly do some specialist medal reference books.

The author and his wife, during a trip to Paris in the Spring of 1988, visited the Musée National de la Légion d'Honneur et Ordres de Chevalerie. On display was a Croix de Guerre with nineteen such palms on the ribbon. This seems to confirm that it was not of a particularly high status; and ties in with what the author of a medal catalogue wrote, that so many Croix de Guerre were issued that it was not highly thought of as an award. It will be noted that *The London Gazette* does not specify what classes of the decoration were being awarded.

Lawrence came in for a Mention in Despatches by General Wingate, in his Despatch No. 2. dated 15th June 1918, and published in the *Fifth Supplement to The London Gazette* dated 15th December 1919, pages 15608-15610, when he notes:

'4. In the meantime, early in July [1917], as a result of an operation, brilliantly planned and executed by Captain Lawrence, Akaba, the last position on the Hedjaz Coast held by the Turks, was captured; . . .'

Earlier in the Despatch it is mentioned that at time of writing Lawrence was a Lieutenant-Colonel.

It is thus reasonably clear what did constitute the five decorations that Hogarth referred to in his letter of October 1917, mistaken though it has been proved: the Legion of Honour (March 1916), the Silver Medal for Military Valour (August 1916), the Order of the Nile (September 1916), the Companionship of the Bath (June 1917), and the Croix de Guerre (November 1917).

Amongst the appointments announced in the *Second Supplement to The London Gazette*, number 30376, dated 12th November, 1917, page 11657, there was entered:

'*General Staff.*
G.S.O., 2nd Grade.-Temp. Maj. T. E. Lawrence, C.B., Gen. List. 1st Oct. 1917.'

Then in a HOME LETTER to his parents dated 14th December 1917 he stated that:

'. . . they have just raised my pay, by pushing me up the roll of Staff appointments. I'm now called a G.S.O.2.

The French Government has stuck another medal on to me: a croix de guerre this time. I wish they would not bother, but they never consult one before doing these things. At least I have never accepted one, and will never wear one or allow one to be conferred on me openly. One cannot do more, for these notices are published in the Press first thing, and to counter-announce that one refused it, would create more publicity than the award itself. I am afraid you will be rather disgusted, but it is not my fault, and by lying low and simply not taking the things when given me, I avoid ever really getting them.'

There is conflicting evidence as to what eventually happened to Lawrence's Croix de Guerre medal. In *T.E.LAWRENCE BY HIS FRIENDS*, page 301, his brother A. W. Lawrence commented:

'As a matter of fact, he returned the decorations sent him by other governments, with the exception of the Croix de Guerre of France, which he sent around the streets of Oxford on the neck of Hogarth's dog.'

It has been suggested, however, that it was more likely to have been the Legion of Honour: the only decoration Lawrence apparently confessed to have kept.
     And again, in *T.E.LAWRENCE TO HIS BIOGRAPHERS:GRAVES*, page 107, Lawrence is said to have returned his decorations to their donors.
     Then, in *T.E.LAWRENCE TO HIS BIOGRAPHERS:LIDDELL HART*, page 157, he handed his Croix de Guerre back (in November 1918) to Colonel Brémond; and on page 373 there is Lawrence's further comment that this was done:

'*not because of the rebuff, but to follow up my return of British decorations.*'

     Arthur Russell, who was at Bovington at the same time as Lawrence, has also stated that Lawrence had told him that medals had been thrown over a London bridge, which is borne out by the following. In the Codrington Library at All Souls, Oxford, is a letter of Lawrence to Lionel Curtis, dated 22nd February 1929, in which he asked (perhaps not wholly seriously) if he should throw the third of his daggers, should he retrieve it from its then possessor:

'*off Lambeth Bridge into the Thames, to lie with my decorations for some dredger of the future.*'

     But according to statements in a scrapbook in St. Martin's church, Wareham, made by John Stephen M.M., who was also with Lawrence at Bovington:

'*In his [Lawrence's] chest at the end of his bed were all his medals as he lifted up the lid. He refused to wear any because British Governemnt refused to honour their treaties which he was part of.*'

     It has often been commented by his contemporaries that Lawrence was careless about his mode of army dress during the WW1 period, and that he never wore any medal ribbons on his uniform at anytime since. Certainly no known photographs seem to exist showing him wearing any decorations or even ribbons.
     Writing from Cairo on the 23rd December 1917, a fortnight after the capture of Jerusalem on the 9th, D.G.Hogarth wrote to his wife concerning Lawrence, and quoted in Brown and Cave's *A TOUCH OF GENIUS*, page 108:

'*He went about happily in a second lieutenant's tunic and badges somewhere between a lieutenant and a captain, and no decorations and no belt. When he went to Jerusalem with Allenby [on the 11th] he is reported to have borrowed from one person and another a regular staff outfit with proper badges and even decorations.*

I only hope he appears in the cinema pictures taken on that occasion, because, otherwise, an unknown aspect of him will be lost.'

Lawrence himself recorded in the *SEVEN PILLARS*, Chapter LXXXI, that Allenby:

'was good enough, although I had done nothing for the success, to let Clayton [Brigadier-General Sir Gilbert Clayton, and one of Lawrence's chiefs during the Desert Campaign] take me along as a staff officer of the day. The personal Staff tricked me out in their spare clothes till I looked like a Major of the British Army. Dalmeny lent me red tabs, Evans his brass hat; so that I had the gauds of my appointment in the ceremony of the Jaffa gate, which for me was the supreme moment of the war.'

Colonel Wavell, who walked beside Lawrence in the triumphal procession, later wrote in *T.E.LAWRENCE BY HIS FRIENDS*, page 147:

'He was gay that day, with jests at his borrowed uniform and at the official appointment that had been loaned to him for the ceremony - staff officer to Bertie Clayton.'

In the event, Lawrence does appear for brief moments in the resulting poor quality film taken on that occasion. In *A TOUCH OF GENIUS* by Brown and Cave, page 108, there is a blown-up still from the film, clearly showing Lawrence, but very little detail of uniform decoration - though he is shown wearing leather leggings and a Sam-Browne belt. (This particular film footage had been included in the two videos that had been compiled for sale to T.E.Lawrence Society members in the Society's early days.) Of course, it must be remembered that those were still relatively early days of the cinematograph, and clarity (especially away from film studios) was still leaving a lot to be desired, particularly in harsh and dusty Middle Eastern light; plus the subsequent deterioration of film from that period.

Regarding Lawrence and his general mode of dress, in *T.E.LAWRENCE BY HIS FRIENDS*, page 160, Captain T. Henderson mentioned that:

'As he had difficulty somehow in obtaining the requisite hat-badge, well, he just didn't bother.'

Known photographs of the period show Lawrence thus badgeless.

For his part in the successful defensive battle of Tafilah against the Turks, on the 25th January 1918, Lawrence was awarded by Britain with the Distinguished Service Order (D.S.O.). The citation reproduced in the *Third Supplement to The London Gazette*, number 30681, of 13th May 1918, page 5694, stated:

'T./Maj. Thomas Edward Lawrence, C.B., Spec. List.

For conspicuous gallantry and devotion to duty in an engagement. He showed splendid leadership and skill, and was largely responsible for the success of the action in which 300 prisoners, two field guns, and twenty-three machine guns were captured.'

The badge of the D.S.O. consists of a gold cross patée, enamelled white, edged with gold, having in the centre of the obverse, within a wreath of laurel enamelled green, a gold Imperial Crown, upon a red enamelled field. On the reverse, within a similar wreath and on a similar red field is the Royal Cypher of George V - GvR - surmounted by a small crown. The badge is suspended from a bar ornamented with laurel. The ribbon is red with narrow blue borders, which itself is further suspended from a brooch bar. Unfortunately this is another decoration where the enamelling is liable to chipping. The badge is not marked with the name of the recipient, and is not returnable on the death of the recipient.

This award was introduced in 1886, mainly to reward officers for acts of gallantry which were not quite in the same class as deeds for which the Victoria Cross would be merited, and to overcome difficulties that arose with awards of the C.B. and resultant accelerated promotions. After 1914 it tended to be confined to officers of the (equivalent) rank of major and above. As regards its position in the Order of Precedence, it comes quite low down the list, being sixth below that of his C.B.

In one of his *HOME LETTERS*, that from Cairo dated 8th March 1918, Lawrence had earlier written:

'They have now given me a D.S.O. It's a pity all this good stuff is not sent to someone who would use it! Also apparently I'm a colonel of sorts. Don't make any change in my address of course.'

In *T.E.LAWRENCE TO HIS BIOGRAPHERS:GRAVES*, page 93, Lawrence comments that this promotion also made him a Staff Officer Grade 1. His official appointment as a Temporary Lieutenant-Colonel was on 12th March 1918, but it was not until in the *Second Supplement to The London Gazette*, number 30773, of 1st July 1918, page 7715, would be found:

'Commands And Staff.
Special Appointments.
(Graded for purposes of pay as G.S.O's., 1st Grade.)-12th Mar. 1918.
Temp. Maj. T. E. Lawrence, C.B., D.S.O., Gen. List, and to be temp. Lt.-Col.
whilst so empld.'

And again in the *Army List*, still listed under 'Majors' from August 1918 until
December 1919, there is the additional side note:

'Lawrence *T.E. C.B. D.S.O. (F) Lt.Col. (whilst holding Spec. Appt. 12th March
1918) 5th August 1917. Whilst specially employed.'

In other words, a temporary Major from 5th August 1917, and presumably an
even more temporary Lieutenant-Colonel from 12th March 1918.
   Only three days after Tafilah, Lawrence and a band of Bedouin uniquely scuttled
a Turkish food transport flotilla on the Dead Sea, near Kerak. As Lawrence was to
mention   to   Graves,   as   recorded   in   *T.E.LAWRENCE   TO   HIS
BIOGRAPHERS:GRAVES*, page 97:

'One of the two occasions in British Miltary history. I recommended myself,
vainly, for a naval D.S.O. after this engagement.'

   This is somewhat incorrect in that there was no such separate naval award, and a
mistake compounded by also being said erroneously to have a different coloured
ribbon. He could, though, have received a bar to his existing D.S.O. Headquarters
however saw through Lawrence's joke, and awarded nothing.
   Then in July 1918, whilst on a reconnaissance ride, in spite of having made the
regulation 'friendly' signal, Lawrence and his party were attacked by a couple of
British aeroplanes, but refrained from retaliation with their own twenty automatic
rifles. According to *T.E.LAWRENCE TO HIS BIOGRAPHERS*, pages 101 and
127, when later reporting this incident to Air Vice-Marshal Sir Geoffrey Salmond,
Lawrence this time ironically recommended himself for the Distinguished Flying
Cross (D.F.C.):

'for presence of mind in not shooting down two Bristol Fighters.'

   The D.F.C., just recently instituted in June 1918, would of course have only
been awarded to Royal Flying Corps personnel, and then for actual flying
operations. The alternating violet and white stripes on the medal ribbon at that
time were horizontal: becoming the current diagonal a little later.

In Chapter CIII of *SEVEN PILLARS OF WISDOM*, Lawrence wrote in referring to his thirtieth birthday on 16th August 1918:

'It came to me queerly how, four years ago, I had meant to be a general and knighted, when thirty. Such temporal dignities (if I survived the next four weeks) were now in my grasp - only that my sense of the falsity of the Arab position had cured me of crude ambition: while it left me my craving for good repute among men . . . Contempt for my passion for distinction made me refuse every offered honour.'

In the *Fifth Supplement to The London Gazette*, number 30939, of 4th October 1918, page 11813, amongst the names brought to the notice of the Secretary of State for War for valuable services rendered in connection with Military Operations in Hedjaz, was:

'Staff.
Lawrence, Maj. (T.Lt.-Col) T. E., C.B., D.S.O., Gen. List.'

Another card was to be completed at the M.O.D. for this occurrence, now also at the National Archives, reading:

'LAWRENCE, T.E. Maj. (T/Lt.Col.) C.B., D.S.O.
Gen. List.
Staff.
M.I.D. L.G.7.10.18 page 11813'

Somewhat belatedly the *Supplement to The London Gazette*, number 31686, of 12th December 1919, page 15553, reported:

'Commands And Staff.
  The undermentioned relinquish their appts.:-
Special Appointments.
Cl. X.-Temp. Maj. T. E. Lawrence, C.B., D.S.O., and relinquishes the temp. rank of Lt.-Col. 16th Oct. 1918.'

- but see *The London Gazette* of 11th May 1920.
  We only have Lawrence's word for it that immediately after the capture of Damascus on 2nd October 1918, which more or less ended the Desert Campaign, as quoted from Lawrence in *T.E.LAWRENCE TO HIS BIOGRAPHERS:GRAVES*, page 93 and 165):

'My odd pip, to full Colonel, came when I wanted to return to England after Damascus. I went to G.H.Q. and asked for the promotion. They were surprised. I explained it was to get a berth on the Staff train through Italy. So they told me to put it up - special, temporary, acting.'

His confirmation of this may be found in *T.E.LAWRENCE TO HIS BIOGRAPHERS:LIDDELL HART*, page 165. In addition to putting up the additional pip on each shoulder, one wonders whether he also bothered to put up the appropriate red lapel tabs, etc., as he apparently did earlier at Jerusalem.

AFTER THE DESERT CAMPAIGN

Recognition of Lawrence's contribution to the defeat of the Turks continued for some time after the War. In a Despatch dated 27th December 1918 to the War Office from General Wingate, General Officer Commanding, Hedjaz - which was subsequently published in the *Fifth Supplement to The London Gazette*, number 31690, 12th December 1919, on page 15611 may be read:

'8. . . . These operations of the Northern Arab Army [immediately leading-up to its entry into Damascus], in which Lieut.-Colonel T. E. Lawrence played so distinguished a rôle . . .'

As we have seen, Lawrence had been gazetted for the Companionship of the Bath in 1917, and the Distinguished Service Order in January 1918. But up until October 1918 he had seemingly not been physically invested with them. During the war King George V had taken a personal interest in Lawrence's activities, as shown in the Royal Archives (see Tunbridge). Thus a private audience was arranged at Buckingham Palace on the 20th or 30th October, (biographers mention either date), when King George V took that opportunity to bestow the insignia of these two decorations. However, Lawrence politely wished to be excused, saying that he had pledged his word about Arab independence to Emir Faisal, and that now the British Government were about to let the Arabs down. According to Lawrence in a letter to E. L. Greenhill dated 20th March, (quoted in Tabachnick's *IMAGES OF LAWRENCE*, page 22,) he recalled:

'as for decorations: I resigned 'em all into H.M.'s own hands: he was nearly moved to tears.'

Another version may be found on pages 130/131 of *T.E.LAWRENCE TO HIS BIOGRAPHERS:LIDDELL HART.*

'Re decorations with George V.
About December 1918. Before he went to see Feisal at Marseilles. Had told the Military Secretary that he would not take any decorations, but the latter failed to warn the King. Thus T.E. had to explain again . . . (T.E. had told Allenby first of all when Allenby said that he had put T.E. in for a "K", and Allenby had wired T.E. home.)'

The "K" was a knighthood - an upgrading of his C.B. to Knight Commander of the most Honourable Order of the Bath (K.C.B.). With this a military badge (larger than that of the Companionship of the Bath - *q.v.*) is worn suspended from its crimson ribbon around the neck, with in addition a star on the left breast. The military star is in the shape of a silver cross pattée, superimposed in the centre by a device similar to that of the military badge. In the Order of Precedence the K.C.B. would have shot Lawrence some little way into the top half of the list.

According to Mack in his *A PRINCE OF OUR DISORDER*, page 257, someone else who was present at the time of this private audience noted:

'During the conversation, Colonel Lawrence said that he had pledged his word to Feisal, and that now the British Government were about to let down the Arabs over the Sykes-Picot Agreement. He was an Emir among the Arabs and intended to stick to them through thick and thin and, if necessary, fight against the French for the recovery of Syria.

Colonel Lawrence said that he did not know that he had been gazetted or what the etiquette was in such matters, but he hoped the King would forgive any want of courtesy on his part in not taking these decorations.'

In *T.E.LAWRENCE TO HIS BIOGRAPHERS:GRAVES*, page 107, it was revealed:

'According to information given me by Lawrence in 1920, and noted down not long after . . . The King did not at first understand his refusal of a K.C.B. [Knight Commander of the Bath - *sic*] and thought he was aiming higher; so offered him an O.M. [Order of Merit]. When Lawrence refused even that, he sighed resignedly and said, "Well, there's one vacant: I suppose it will have to go to Foch." Lawrence made no reply but was amused at the irony of [the French Marshal] Foch being given what he refused.'

Whatever exactly did transpire at that audience, the unprecedented incident naturally caused quite a stir in official circles, though the King (not having been previously appraised of Lawrence's opinions) apparently took it in good part. This episode has also been variously covered elsewhere, for example by Winston Churchill in his *GREAT CONTEMPORARIES*.

A photograph of King George V, together with his Private Secretary, Lord Stamfordham, who was present on that occasion, is included amongst this monograph's illustrations.

The Order of Merit was instituted in 1902, being awarded very rarely to officers of the fighting services and to civilians for very distinguished and conspicuous services either in peace or war. The badge consists of a gold cross, pattée convexed, enamelled red, edged in blue, with, in the centre of the obverse, the words **FOR MERIT** on a blue ground. In the centre of the reverse is the Royal cypher. The cross is surmounted by a Tudor crown, and is worn around the neck from a 50mm-wide ribbon, half blue, half crimson.

Armed service recipients of the Order have additionally two silver crossed swords between the arms of the cross in their badge - see illustration. Recipients have the right to use the letters 'O.M.' after their names. Lawrence visited the Dorset novelist and poet Thomas Hardy many times between 1923-1926, and doubtless saw his host's civilian version of this Order awarded him in 1910. The O.M. ranked seventh in the Order of Precedence, so that Hardy would have greatly outranked Lawrence; and would still have done so even if the latter had accepted a K.C.B., though it might well have amused them if both had the O.M.

So in the event, these were all yet further decorations that Lawrence was never to wear.

He would during the course of the War have qualified for the '1914-1915 Star', which was sanctioned by Army Order 20 of 1919, awarded for service during the period 5th August 1914 to 31st December 1915. It was 1¾ inches wide, and 2½ inches from top to bottom, being made of bronze. In the centre of the star was a scroll with the inscription 1914-15 surrounded by a laurel wreath at the bottom of which is a G, whilst across the face are two crossed swords; near the suspension a crown. The reverse is plain, with engraved in block capitals is the service number (though not for officers), rank, name and unit of the recipient. The ribbon was 1¼ inches wide, being red, white and blue shaded and watered.

Lawrence would also have automatically qualified for both the British War Medal and the Victory Medal, sanctioned respectively by Army Order 266 of 1919 and Army Order 301 of 1919.

The War Medal was awarded to all personnel who had been on active service for some period during the war, and to record the bringing of the war to a successful conclusion. It was struck in silver, being 1·42 inches in diameter, with the obverse a coinage head of George V, and bearing the legend

GEORGIVS V BRITT : OMN : REX ET IND : IMP

On the reverse is St. George on horseback trampling on the shield of the Central Powers, and at the bottom a skull and crossbones and at the top a sun, with around the edge **1914** and **1918**. Faintly indented on the rim would be the service number (not for officers), rank, name and unit of the recipient in block capitals. The suspension was straight and non swivel from a 1¼ inch wide ribbon which had an orange centre stripe, watered with stripes of white and black on each side and with borders of royal blue.

The Victory Medal was of bronze, being 1·42 inches in diameter, and rimless. On the obverse was the winged figure of 'Victory' with the left arm extended, and in her right hand a palm branch; whilst on the reverse the inscription **THE**

GREAT WAR FOR CIVILISATION 1914-1919 surrounded by a wreath. There was a ring suspender, with the ribbon 1·55 inches wide, being watered from the centre red and on both sides yellow, green, blue and violet shaded to form the colours of two rainbows. The reipient's particulars were again faintly impressed in block capitals on the rim.

This group of three WW1 campaign medals were to become commonly known as 'Pip, Squeak and Wilfred' - the names of a daily newspaper's three famous cartoon animal characters, whose antics were certainly continuing to be published up until the beginning of WW2.

As we have already seen, Lawrence had been 'Mentioned in Despatches' a number of times. A final one can be found in the *Sixth Supplement to The London Gazette*, number 31249, of 24th March 1919, page 3866; for amongst the names brought to the Secretary of State for War for valuable services rendered in connection with the Military Operations in Arabia, was:

'Lawrence, T./Lt.-Col. T. E., C.B., D.S.O., Spec. List.'

In 1920 King George V was to give approval for an emblem to be worn on the riband of the WW1 Victory Medal to denote a person having been so mentioned. The emblem was to take the form of a small multiple leaved bronze oak leaf, affixed to the centre of the medal ribbon at an angle of 60° from the inside edge of the ribbon, stem to the right. A smaller version of this oak leaf was placed transversely across the ribbon worn on the uniform when the medal itself was not worn. Only one oak leaf was to be worn, irrespective of the number of times the holder of the medal had been mentioned in despatches - unlike the French with their Croix de Guerre, as has already been noticed.

Officers had to personally apply for their campaign medals, and thus it is to be expected that Lawrence would not have ever claimed his. They do not appear on his medal cards in the National Archives.

During the first half of 1919 he was assisting the Arab delegation at the Paris Peace Conference. Ralph H. Isham said in *T.E.LAWRENCE BY HIS FRIENDS*, page 294, that he was first introduced to Lawrence in the summer of 1919, when the latter was:

'in a very new uniform, which bore no ribbons; (with the) insignia of Lieutenant-Colonel on his uniform.'

According to Tunbridge, Lawrence was formally struck off the strength of the E.E.F. [Egyptian Expeditionary Force] on 15th June 1919 (Auth DAG - ECH

A(D)82/1). But in the *Fourth Supplement to The London Gazette*, number 31898, of 11th May 1920, there was a correction to an earlier *London Gazette*:

'Commands And Staff.
The undermentioned relinquish their appts.:-
Special Appointments.
Cl. X.-The date of the relinquishment of his appt. and the temp. rank of Lt.-Col. by temp. Maj. T. E. Lawrence, C.B., D.S.O., is 1st Aug. 1919, and not as in the Gazette of 12th Dec. 1919.'

(Number 31686 which gave a date of 16th Oct. 1918.)
There was a follow-up to this in the *Third Supplement to The London Gazette*, number 31932, dated 7th June 1920, page 6326:

Memoranda.
'The undermentioned to be temp. Lt.-Cols.:-
Whilst specially empld.:-
Temp. Maj. T. E. Lawrence, C.B., D.S.O., Gen. List, from 16th Oct. 1918 to 31st July 1919. (Substituted for the notification in the Gazette of 13th May 1920.)

Although 1st August 1919 is thus the official date of demobilisation after completion of his involvement in the Paris Peace Conference, according to *T.E.LAWRENCE TO HIS BIOGRAPHERS:GRAVES*, page 108 it was "In July 1919". But it might also be inferred to have been 1st September 1919, for writing this day from his home at 2 Polstead Road, Oxford, Lawrence wrote:

"I'm out of the Army today: . . ."

and according to Brown's *LETTERS OF T.E.LAWRENCE*, pages 168 *et seq*, he repeatedly thereafter told people not to call him Colonel.
Because he had been gazetted for both his C.B. and D.S.O. awards - although refusing acceptance of the actual insignia - Lawrence was still officially recognised and advertised as possessing them. For example, as his part in Winston Churchill's initiative for the Cairo Peace Conference in 1922, Lawrence was appointed in June 1921 a plenipotentiary under the great seal of England, with full powers to treat with King Hussein, Grand Sherif of Mecca, who had originally started the Arab Revolt in 1916. According to Garnett's *LETTERS OF T.E.LAWRENCE*, page 332, this document, dated 30th June 1921, was addressed:

'Our most trusty and well-beloved Thomas Edward Lawrence Esquire, Lieutenant
Colonel in our Army, Companion of Our Most Honourable Order of the Bath,
Companion of Our Distinguished Service Order.'

Editions of *The London Gazette* following the end of the war had contained
lists of officers relinquishing their commissions on completion of service,
together with what rank subsequently granted or retained. Nothing has been
found in this respect concerning Lawrence.

Finally, what other 'Eastern decorations' might Lawrence have been awarded?
From the end of 1919, and well into 1920, *The London Gazette* carried details of
those British personnel awarded the 'Order of al Nahada (Ouisam Amn Nahada)
by the kingdom of the Hejaz'. Amongst those mentioned were General Allenby
with the highest class "with brilliants" in the *Supplement to The London
Gazette*, number 31812, dated 8th March 1920, page 2870; and Captain V. D.
Siddons with a fourth class Nahada (*Supplement to The London Gazette*,
number 31847, dated 1st April 1920, page 4022) of the Royal Flying Corps, who
flew Lawrence about during the Desert Campaign a few times, and being
mentioned in *SEVEN PILLARS OF WISDOM*). It could thus have been
expected that should Lawrence also have been awarded one he would have had a
second class. But no notice has been found in *The London Gazette* of him being
so awarded.

However, in letters to the author dated 28th October 1988 and 16th June 1989,
from historian and writer Suleiman Mousa of Amman, Jordan, it was learned that
Lawrence was granted the Order of Al Nahda, second class, along with several
other British officers who had served alongside the Arabs during the Desert
Campaign. The news of the awards were published in the *Al-Qibleh* newspaper
No. 320 dated 9 Muharram 1338 H (7th October 1919). Mr Mousa was not able
to provide further information because the records of the Hashemite Kingdom of
Hejaz were left in Mecca, because King Hussein Bin Ali was obliged to leave it in
haste, as a result of the Saudi attack in September 1924.

This Order was instituted by King Hussein just after WW1, to commemorate the
renaissance of the Arab kingdom. It had five classes, with the first two having a
sash and breast star. The sash was green with narrow stripes of black, green, white
and red. The Nahada badge was an elaborate six-pointed star in tracery and green
enamel. In the centre were two crossed flags in colour on a gold ground
surrounded by an Arabic inscription in gold on a red-enamelled circle. The flags
each consisted of horizontal black-green-white bands indented with a red triangle
- in other words the official flag of the Arab Revolt from June 1917. The ribbon
worn on the uniform is of black, white and green segments, with the wider central
white one divided by a narrow red bar.

Illustrated in this monograph is the 'Nahada - 4th Class', with its arabic citation, awarded to Captain S. H. Brodie, who had also served with Lawrence in the desert, and was mentioned in *SEVEN PILLARS OF WISDOM*. The accompanying Arabic Citation and its translation are also reproduced.

Reference books listing the awards and decorations of various people, show Lawrence being only credited with the C.B., the D.S.O., and the Legion of Honour. As Brodie is shown credited with his Nahda, this seems to confirm that Lawrence was not in fact subsequently awarded one - it being equally safe to assume that he had refused his, as he did other awards, and had been able to stop it being officially listed in *The London Gazette*.

In the case of Foreign Orders, circular rosettes can be worn on the riband to denote the class of Order. In addition to the rosette on the riband, an example of the rosette may be also worn in the lapel-slot while the wearer is in everyday civilian dress. To denote the multiple classes of an Order, a coloured flash or knot is often used protruding from each side behind the rosette, the colours of the flash being: 1st class - all gold; 2nd class (Lawrence's Nahda) - half gold, half silver; 3rd clas - all silver; 4th class - no flash; 5th class - lapel clip narrow riband (as instanced with the Legion of Honour). A rosette worn on the full size medal riband will denote that the Order is a 4th class award as opposed to the 5th class award as more often than not the actual badge will be the same size and design.

One can only speculate as to whether the subject was raised (certainly not by Lawrence himself) about his earlier presumed refusal to accept Hussein's 'Order of the Nahda' when the two met for negotiations in mid-1921.

During the T.E.Lawrence Society's trip to Jordan in May 1989, it was noted that the hotel used by the party in Akaba was situated in Al Nahda Street.

In *T.E.LAWRENCE BY HIS FRIENDS*, page 165, Captain Brodie gave another amusing vignette of Lawrence and his casual mode of dress and behaviour, on Cairo railway station:

'Lawrence passed everyone looking neither to right nor left, did not salute his superior officers nor return the salute given him by the Tommies. His dress was a cap without a badge, his hair a bit longer than regulation length, protruding well out from under it, a serge jacket with slack trousers, a red tie, no Sam-Browne belt, a pair of light patent leather shoes, a 'pip' on one shoulder and a 'pip' and crown on the other.'

A study of the group photograph of Faisal with some of the delegates and advisers at the 1919 Peace Conference, shows Lawrence in Lieutenant-Colonel's uniform, wearing his arab head-dress, and yet again minus any medal ribands - unlike some other members of the party.

After he eventually became King of Iraq in 1922, Faisal naturally instituted a few decorations. In a letter dated 9th October 1928, (quoted in Brown's *LETTERS OF T.E.LAWRENCE*, page 383), to the new British High Commissioner and Commander-in-Chief for Iraq, (Brigadier-General Sir Gilbert Clayton), Lawrence wrote:

'*I laughed when I read of his [Feisal] instituting the Order of the Two Rivers [Order of Al Rafidhain] . . . I nearly wrote and asked for one of his stars, to put on my hitherto empty coat. After all, I'm almost a foundation-member of his kingdom.*'

There were three classes of this Order, with separate military and civil ribands. Both ribands were red, but the military version had a narrow black band at each end and a thick central one, whilst the civilian one had just a narrow black band near each end. As he seems to have considered having the decoration for his specific services in the 1921 Cairo Conference when helping to set up the kingdom of Iraq, Lawrence might have therefore been awarded either version, though it is the 2nd class military version that is illustrated in this monograph. The circular star of this decoration had seven extending red points terminating in small golden globes, the centre of the obverse consisting of a superimposed wreath in green and white enamel surrounding a white circle having an Arabic inscription. In the centre is a gold crown on a blue background. The reverse is the same seven red points superimposed over which which is a white enamel circle having an Arabic inscription, and in the centre a gold Arabic inscription on a gold background. The star is suspended from its ribbon (which has a gold royal Hashemite crown on it) by a gold laurel wreath, with two crossed Arabian sword superimposed upon it - see illustration.

During his short first period of R.A.F. service, commencing in 1922, and his subsequent period in the Tank Corps from 1923 to 1926, and the short period thereafter at R.A.F. Cranwell, Lawrence would not have qualified for any further awards. Then when stationed with the R.A.F. in India, from January 1927 until forced to leave because of adverse Press headline publicity in December 1928, he would not have qualified for the India General Service Medal. This was only issued with named bars for specific engagements - and he just happened to be there in-between-times.

Lawrence would not have obtained the R.A.F.'s Long Service & Good Conduct Medal, for which the qualifying period of unbroken armed forces' service with good character is 15 years. He had joined the Tank Corps in March 1923, and retired from the R.A.F. in March 1935, thus giving him just 12 years continuous service.

POSTSCRIPT

We have finally come to see the truth in the moral about 'not believing everything one reads in a newspaper'. Whilst the original newspaper report must therefore have been false: if it had been true it may be agreed that it would have been a typical and worthy addition to the Lawrence legend.

In the same vein, many so-called reminiscences of personnel who said they served with, or knew Lawrence: their stories too should be treated with a degree of caution, or even scepticism.

It would have been at a weekend in July 1989 that some members of the T.E.Lawrence Society met at the Bovington home of the late Roland A. Hammersley DFM, who was a founder member and first Chairman of the Society. The occasion was to celebrate Roland's 67th birthday. The author took that opportunity to wear his collection of certain and spurious awards that Lawrence could have worn. To aid to the authenticity he also wore an arab head-dress he had purchased earlier that year during a Society 'Lawrence Trail' in Jordan. See illustration.

This monograph ends with a final Lawrentian quote. At the end of his contribution to the posthumous book *T.E.LAWRENCE BY HIS FRIENDS*, page 94, Leonard Woolley wrote with reference to Lawrence:

'He once said to me, after the War, that the stroke of humour which had pleased him most was that when he refused other decorations he accepted the Legion of Honour.'

BIBLIOGRAPHY

Abbott, P.E. & Tamplin, J.M.A. *BRITISH GALLANTRY AWARDS* Guinness
                                            Superlatives Ltd/B.A.Seaby Ltd 1971
Angus, Ian *MEDALS AND DECORATIONS* Ward Lock 1973
Brown, Malcolm & Cave, Julia *A TOUCH OF GENIUS* Dent 1988
Churchill, W.S. *GREAT CONTEMPORARIES* Reprint Society 1941
Connelly, Stephen *SPINK'S GUIDE TO THE WEARING OF ORDERS,*
                        DECORATIONS AND MEDALS Spink & Son Ltd 1986
Dixon, Alec *TINNED SOLDIER* Jonathan Cape 1941
Dorling, H.Taprell *RIBBONS AND MEDALS* George Philip & Son 1974
Gordon, Lawrence L. *BRITISH ORDERS AND AWARDS* L.L.Gordon 1959
Hart, Basil Liddell *T.E.LAWRENCE: IN ARABIA AND AFTER* Cape 1934
Knightley, P. & Simpson, C. *THE SECRET LIVES OF LARENCE OF*
                                                          ARABIA Nelson 1969
The London Gazette website <www.gazette-online.co/archivesearch>
Nichols, G.W. 'Some Notes On The Military Career Of T.E.Lawrence'
                        T.E.Lawrence Studies NEWSLETTER, Vol.1, No. 2. 1981-2
LAWRENCE, T.E. THE LETTERS OF (ed. Garnett) Cape 1938
LAWRENCE, T.E. THE HOME LETTERS OF Blackwell 1954
LAWRENCE, T.E. THE LETTERS OF (ed. Brown) Dent 1988
Lawrence, T.E. *SEVEN PILLARS OF WISDOM* Various editions
Lawrence, T.E. *THE MINT* Cape 1955
LAWRENCE, T.E. TO HIS BIOGRAPHERS, GRAVES AND LIDDELL
                                                          HART Cassell 1963
Poulsom, N.W. *A CATALOGUE OF CAMPAIGN AND INDEPENDENCE*
        MEDALS ISSUED DURING THE TWENTIETH CENTURY TO THE
                        BRITISH ARMY Corbitt & Hunter 1969
Purves, Alec A. *COLLECTING MEDALS and DECORATIONS* B.A.Seaby
                                                                                      1978
Tabachnick, S.E. (ed.) *THE T.E.LAWRENCE PUZZLE* University of Georgia
                                                                                      1984
Tabachnick, S.E. & Matheson, C. *IMAGES OF LAWRENCE* Cape 1988
Thomas, Lowell *WITH LAWRENCE IN ARABIA* Hutchinson 1925
Tunbridge, Paul *WITH LAWRENCE IN THE ROYAL AIR FORCE*
                                            Buckland Publications Ltd 2000
Winstone, H.V.F. (ed.) *THE DIARIES OF PARKER PASHA* Quartet Boooks
                                                                                      1983
Woolley, C.L. *DEAD TOWNS & LIVING MEN* Cape 1932
Yardley, Michael *BACKING INTO THE LIMELIGHT* Harrap 1985

The T. E. LAWRENCE SOCIETY

(Registered Charity No. 297940)

The Society was formed in 1985, (the 50th anniversary of Lawrence's death), to promote his memory; and to enable individual members to meet, participate and develop their interests, and further their knowledge by research into his life. The Society soon after became a registered educational charity. Membership is now world-wide, with representation from the five continents.

Members engage in projects such as collecting memorabilia, and interviewing the decreasing number of people who remember Lawrence. Individual interests range from collecting books, academic literature, ephemera, to motorcycles. There is ample scope for everyone's talents in the various activities of the Society. There are two or three local groups of members.

The Society arranges lectures; organised visits to places connected with Lawrence, such as his birthplace at Tremadog in North Wales, Oxford, Bovington Camp and his cottage at Clouds Hill in Dorset, R.A.F. Mount Batten, and Jordan where many of his desert actions took place. A 2-3 day Symposium is held every two years with a diverse programme of speakers and lecture topics.

A *NEWSLETTER* is published quarterly, as well as a bi-annual *JOURNAL*. Several members are also authors, with a continuing output of Lawrence related published works.

The Society has a comprehensive library and archival collection housed at the Central Library in Oxford; as well as a collection of books at the Wareham Public Library, and artifacts on display at Bovington Tank Museum - both in Dorset.

The Society has a website <www.telsociety.org> with both public access and a members' only section. This gives details of how to join the Society; or enquiries can be made by writing to:

The T. E. Lawrence Society
P.O. Box 728
Oxford OX2 9ZJ

Ronald Knight was born in Portsmouth, Hampshire, in 1932, but for well over half his life has lived and worked in Dorset, where he is now retired.

He first had his interest in 'Lawrence of Arabia' aroused when aged 7½, by reading stories about him in a Childrens' Annual.

Except for a couple of visits to Clouds Hill in the mid-1950's, his interest remained dormant. It was awakened in 1984 with the impending 50th anniversary of Lawrence's tragic death, and resulted in the publication the following year of his first work on Lawrence - *Colonel T. E. Lawrence visits Mr. & Mrs. Thomas Hardy.*

He joined the T.E.Lawrence Society soon after its formation in 1985, becoming its chairman in 1986 until 1990. He is now one of the Society's Trustees, as well as having been honoured with an Honorary Membership.